Cat and Dog Make Biggest, Best Sandwich

Let's make a cheese sandwich.
First, take a slice of bread.
Next, put some cheese on it.

Then, put another slice of bread on top.

Wait a minute!
Let's make a *big* cheese sandwich.

First, take a *big* slice of bread.
Next, put a *big* slice of cheese on it.

Then, put another slice of bread on top.

Wait a minute!
Let's make a *bigger* cheese sandwich.

First, take a *bigger* slice of bread.
Next, put a *bigger* slice of cheese on it.

Then, put another slice of bread on top.

Wait a minute!
Let's make the *biggest* cheese sandwich.

First, take the *biggest* slice of bread.
Next, put the *biggest* slice of cheese on it.

Then, put another slice of bread on top.

Wait a minute!
Let's make this *biggest* sandwich a *good* sandwich.

First, take the *biggest* slice of bread.
Next, put the *biggest* slice of cheese on it.
Then, put some red tomato on it.

Then, put another slice of bread on top.

Wait a minute!
Let's make this *biggest* sandwich a *better* sandwich.

First, take the *biggest* slice of bread.
Next, put the *biggest* slice of cheese on it.

Then, put some red tomato on it.
Then, put some green pickles on it.

Then, put another slice of bread on top.

Wait a minute!
Let's make this *biggest* sandwich the *best* sandwich.

First, take the *biggest* slice of bread.
Next, put the *biggest* slice of cheese on it.
Then, put some red tomato on it.

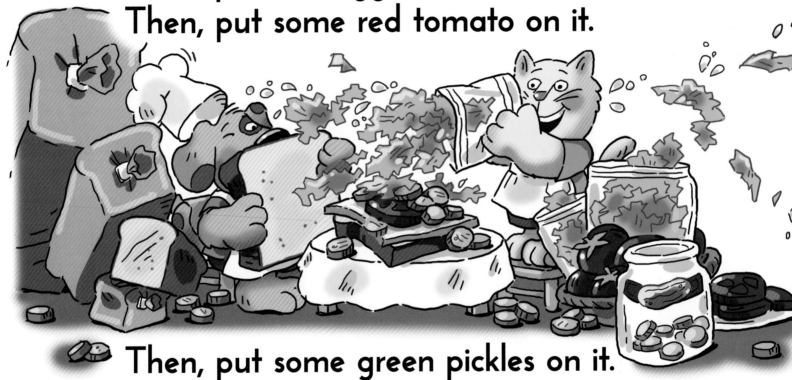

Then, put some green pickles on it.
Then, put some crisp lettuce on it.
Then, put another slice of bread on top.

Yay! We made the biggest, best sandwich of all!

Yum! Let's cut it in half and share it!